Birmingham has always been in a state of change. Even William Hutton, the town's first historian, remarked on this in 1781, forty years after his first visit. A century ago there were still gracious Georgian houses along Colmore Row and a generous sprinkling of peaceful gardens and allotments in the city centre.

A little before, the building of the new stations at Snow Hill and New Street had cleared a lot of squalid, overcrowded old dwellings, when in 1878 Joe Chamberlain, the Lord Mayor, flattened the worst of the slums in cutting Corporation Street, losing at the same time the once elegant Old Square.

Now the onslaught had begun. A host of Victorian public buildings sprang up in the last quarter of the century: the Council House supplanting the quaint row of old houses in Ann Street, the Post Office which replaced Corbett's Temperance Hotel, the Mason College, the Art Gallery — and on the buildings marched. The Victorian city had finally buried the Georgian town.

No sooner had the new buildings settled in than they found the Edwardian age upon them. The packed city was rapidly spreading into local villages — Hall Green, Perry Barr, Yardley, King's Norton — which woke up one morning to find the developers had arrived, and that they had become suburbs, housing estates filling the fields where their horses grazed.

Stream trams had been puffing about the city since 1882 and, with the arrival of the gleaming new electric trams from 1904 and construction of miles of new tramways, the new suburbs were suddenly accessible from the city centre.

This Edwardian extension of the city boundaries trebled its size with more additions as time went on, but after the Second World War the largest redevelopment of all began. I only arrived on the scene at the end of the war, but recall the man in the Bull Ring perpetually struggling out of his chains, the old lady who bawled ''andy carriers' outside 'Woolies', the rustling crabs and live eels in the Market Hall (from 'Fred King the crab king') and the rows of yelling barrow-boys crammed up the cobbled Bull Ring among squashed tomatoes and unruly potatoes. This was the Birmingham most of us remember. Queensways, concrete Bull Rings and bland plate glass have changed all that.

The photographs reproduced in this book are part of the author's collection of postcards and as such do not represent the whole picture. Photos of elegant, tree-lined Handsworth and Edgbaston are common, but little can be seen of the hardships in the slums of Aston. Similarly, there are few postcard images of the enormous variety of trade and industries, changing and developing and forming the basis of Birmingham's growth but, nevertheless, these photographs recall the flavour of the Birmingham many of us knew.

In Edwardian times, the postcard was a means of sending a simple message within a day for ½d, and postcard collecting soon became a highly popular hobby. Every village, town and city was exhaustively photographed and a host of subjects was employed to appease the new collecting mania. It all started in 1902 with the new ½d post but, after the Great War, when postal charges rose to 1d, the postcard fell into disuse, lying in dusty albums for years until the new craze for collecting was revived in the '60s.

Photographs of Birmingham have appeared before, of course, but these pictures are, with the exception of a handful, an original, unpublished collection covering the city centre, the suburbs and a great variety of different aspects of Birmingham life. The period spans from late Victorian times to the Second World War, and for this superb group of photographs I am indebted to many photographers of the day, some known but mostly anonymous.

FRONT COVER: The Bull Ring seen from St Martin's, with an electric tram turning out of Moor Street.

ABOVE: Barges on the Worcester and Birmingham Canal, bringing milk to the Cadbury's factory at Bournville.

A fine study of old New Street with Needless Alley on the right. The date is around 1902 and there is not a motor vehicle in sight. The classical portico up the hill is on the Birmingham Society of Arts building.

New Street from the junction with High Street; King Edward's Grammar School is on the left, where it remained until 1936 and the move to Edgbaston. The Odeon Cinema now partly occupies the site.

A gathering and procession in Victorian New Street, seen from the Town Hall between 1886, when the Post Office was built, and 1899, when Christchurch was demolished. Christchurch was completed in 1814 and New Street is first mentioned in the 1300s. The buildings which replaced the church were commonly known as Galloways Corner after the Second World War, and were demolished in their turn in 1970.

The Bull Ring market and St Martins Church, which was in such poor repair last century that it was rebuilt in 1875. The market is now over 800 years old. The poster on the right advertises Mrs Langtry at 'The Grand'.

Flower sellers in the Bull Ring early in the century.

A Kitson steam tram passing a horse 'bus in Corporation Street early in the century. The Street was cut in 1876 as part of Joe Chamberlain's 'improvements' and it rid the area of some of the city's most congested and wretched slums.

Colmore Row; the Bluecoat School, facing the east end of the churchyard, was closed in 1930. The Colmore family gave their name to the Row, which was previously known as Ann Street.

High Street, looking towards Dale End and Bull Street. Just out of the picture, on the left, was A. Clements' shop, dealer in old artificial teeth, then Charles Britten's bookshop, William Coe's shoe shop and the city arcade. Then comes Spencer the jeweller, Lipton's the grocers and the Turkish Baths. High Street is the correct name for the Bull Ring, and the street was once the site of the cattle market.

Chamberlain Place from Congreve Street, c1905. The fountain and square were opened in 1880 as a tribute to Joe Chamberlain's work when Mayor. The Josiah Mason Science College, at the rear, was built in the late 1870s and became the Mason University College in 1897. Chamberlain had considered developing it into an independent university, but it was decided to build a new one on the Bristol Road, opened in 1909.

The fire in Jamaica Row on 23 March 1906.

The Armistice Day celebrations at the Hall of Memory in Broad Street.

The City Arcade in 1906, built in 1902, connected New Street, High Street and Union Street.

The Market Hall around 1901, with Mr Miles' dining area on the right, was opened in 1835 and cost, with its land, over £73,000. It was bombed in 1940 and demolished in 1960 in the redevelopments. The site is now occupied by the Manzoni Gardens.

The Old Square was developed in the early 1700s, partly on the site of St Thomas's Priory. The area became squalid and overcrowded in Victorian times, and the Square was flattened late in the century when Corporation Street was built. Newbury's shop was taken over by John Lewis in the late 1920s but the open space was kept throughout — even to the present 'Priory Queensway'.

Martineau Street looking towads Corporation Street; Sir Thomas Martineau was Mayor from 1884-1887, as was his father in 1846. The street named after him followed the direction of old 'Crooked Lane', although less tortuously.

Erdington's first tram-car at the Sutton Road terminus in March 1907.

'Win the War' day at Kynoch's — the Witton ammunition factory.

A superb study of a Falcon steam locomotive and trailer on the Moseley route. The top speed for a steam tram was around 15 mph, but they generally rattled and smoked along at far less. In those days there were three companies who leased the tracks from Birmingham Corporation, but by 1914 the Corporation had taken over operation of all the tramways.

A rare photograph of the staff of Arthur Street tram depôt, Coventry Road, in May 1910, when it was the largest in Birmingham, with a capacity for 106 trams.

Mr W. Webb's motor lorry, Stockfield Road, Yardley.

The last Nechells horse tram, running on 30 September 1906. Elsewhere in the city, steam trams had been running from as early as 1882, and the Nechells route was the only one still worked by horses at that time. Ten horse cars had been built especially for the route.

Firemen from the Central Fire Station in Upper Priory in their new motor car.

The driver and conductor of Car 19, with an inspector. This was one of the first batch of electric trams to be built in 1904. In the early days, drivers were open to the elements and were baked or soaked, but the cabs were soon fitted with canvas canopies for protection. This car is on Route 30 — Windmill Lane, Smethwick — and on its way back to town, stopping near the Post Office at Cape Hill (Stewarts the drapers can just be seen through the window).

An unusual view of a tram. This one was returning to its Colmore Row terminus when it crashed.

George Baines delivery vehicles outside the Finch Road 'model bakery' in Lozells. There were 28 Baines shops in the area.

v Motor Bus
rmingham

OPPOSITE: In 1903, the new Milnes-Daimler motor bus, which ran along the Hagley road, was operated by the Birmingham Motor Express Company. ABOVE: The horse tender with 'full turn out' at the Central Fire Station in Upper Priory before the move to Lancaster Place in 1935.

New Street Station was built in 1854 at a cost of £½ million, and later enlarged. Its huge glass and iron roof, supported by rows of columns was, at the time, the largest in the world, with a span of 212 feet. This picture was taken in about 1910. The station retained this appearance until the roof was taken down in 1952.

The Brighton-Eastbourne and South Coast express at LNWR New Street Station in Edwardian times. The footbridge above the train ran from Stephenson Street to Station Street.

GWR Snow Hill was lighter and more efficient than New Street, even though it handled goods as well as passenger trains. The refreshment rooms were probably the best in the country, with walls lined in oak and counters covered in red marble.

The entrance and booking hall of Snow Hill Station in 1912. Notable in the new station were the well-designed buildings and attention to detail like buff terracotta for the cornices, copings, etc, saltglazed bricks facing the walls and white Carrara ware in the ticket office.

Brighton Road Station, built in 1875, with the local down train — 044 tank 1324 of the Midland Railway.

Moseley Station in the early 1920s.

Northfield Station and staff.

Yardley Wood Station entrance in Highfield Road, Hall Green.

OPPOSITE LEFT: *The Chamberlain Clock in Hockley, looking down Vyse Street from Frederick Street in 1914, was erected as a memorial to Joe Chamberlain's work for the British Empire in South Africa and is dated 1903. The chap on the left is wearing the badge of the Birmingham Corporation tramways and, since the clock was a regular boarding point for inspectors, it seems likely that he was just that. RIGHT: Burney Lane, Alum Rock Road, c1904, long before the developers arrived. ABOVE: Victoria Street, Bordesley Green, looking south. On the left is Thomas Henry Baines' bakery shop and on the opposite corner, Fred Corbett's greengrocery business. The tramway was constructed here in 1906, but the dresses are still pre-war.*

Edwardian High Street, King's Heath with Institute Road and the Council School on the right. On the left of the picture are Samuels the hosiers, Chapman and Saunders, stationers and Cariss and Co, auctioneers.

Aston Cross — the new clock tower around 1905. Park Rod is on the left and Lichfield Road on the right.

An early view of the Coventry Road at Hay Mills.

Sparkhill in 1904. The steam tram in the distance is just passing Baker Street on its way to town. Showell Green Lane and Ivor Road are out of the picture to the left.

The old windmill at Yardley Wood stood just outside the city boundary — which ran through the mill pond — and in 1907 was the only mill remaining, although many more existed in early times.

The cockatoos, out for an airing at the Botanic Gardens, Edgbaston in the 1920s.

Green Lane, Hall Green, running from Wake Green Road to Sarehole Road. The cottage and rural lane is still much the same, thanks to the 'green belt'.

The Old Ship Inn, Camp Hill — Prince Rupert's headquarters — photographed in 1868.

The River Rea often flooded. This picture is of Cartland Road, Stirchley and is dated 11 July 1927.

A group of workmen standing outside the Wheatsheaf pub in Sheldon.

Billesley Lane, Moseley in the early 1920s.

Soho Road, Handsworth, with the Council House on the left next to the Fire Station. Photographed c1903, only horse trams and horse drawn vehicles can be seen. The shop on the left — on the corner of Stafford Road — became the Frighted Horse pub in the 1920s.

*An excellent study of Newtown Row and the Barton's Arms taken before the Great War. The Globe picture house
can just be seen on the left, and the Aston Hippodrome on the right is advertising Will Hay and Edna Latonne.*

Tindal Street School, Balsall Heath, celebrating the end of the Great War with buns and orange juice.

Five Ways, Edgbaston, looking down Broad Street, with Islington Row on the right, before the tramway was built in 1913. The statue is that of Joseph Sturge, a philanthropist and slavery abolitionist.

The right hand side of Ladypool Road going towards Stratford Road, between Studley Street and Highgate Road. The first shop is Winfield Bros, gas fitters, plumbers and bell hangers, and next door is Albert Sheldon's sweet shop.

Nechells Green looking down Nechells Place towards Saltley gas works. Bloomsbury Street is on the right and the Beehive pub is on the corner.

Albert Road School, Aston, early this century was between Frederick Road and Albert Road, near the back of Aston swimming baths. Second from the left in the middle row is Fred Done, born in 1900.

Dennis Road School was in Balsall Heath, behind the Drill Hall in Stoney Lane. Its netball team was photographed in 1922.

Happy Valley, Yardley Wood, a popular venue for 'cyclists, campers and picnickers.

Monument Road, Edgbaston, with Perrot's Folly in the distance.

Trotting along the Hagley Road early in the century — before the tramway was built.

Rural Stechford c1905.

Broad Street near Five Ways just before the First World War. The Tilling Stevens TTA II motor 'bus is bound for Quinton and Blackheath.

Selly Oak with Oak Tree Lane on the right, some time before the 1914-18 war. The Rednal motor 'bus is on its way to the Lickey Hills.

Haselucks Green around 1905 before development. The ford at Colebrook Road was a little outside the boundary and Haselucks Green was a quiet country lane.

Saltley College cricket team in 1908.

The Gaiety Theatre in Coleshill Street in March 1914; it started life as the Rodney Inn, which had a hall attached to it and an organ installed in 1846. It was then known as Holders Music Hall but was changed to the Gaiety in 1886. It became a popular theatre, held occasional film shows, was enlarged and later turned into a cinema in 1920. It was rebuilt in 1939 and finally demolished in 1969.

Advertising the 1926 Floral Fête. The prizes were all 'baby cars' (prams) donated by Austins of Corporation Street.

The Springfield Picture Playhouse, Stratford Road, Sparkhill showed its first picture in 1914.

The Royal coach on its way from New Street Station to the new university on the Bristol Road, with an interesting top view of the horse 'bus.

LEFT: Mrs A Findon and Scottie dog outside their shop at 21 Winson Green Road, and RIGHT: Mr F. Jones, the last man to escape alive, photographed at the pithead of Hamstead Colliery after the disaster of 1908.

Yardley Road Sanatorium — the children's section. Tuberculosis was a dread killer around the Great War years especially, and the huge sanatorium was usually well filled.

Erdington Childrens' Home band.

Aston Villa Football Club in 1909. The Club was founded in 1874 as the Wesleyan Football Club, with W.H. Price and George Ramsay as captains, and became professional in 1885. It moved to Villa Park eleven years later, having first played at Wellington Road, Perry Barr.

Messrs Webster and Bullock — meat traders in the market — advertising a sale in aid of wounded soldiers in August 1916.

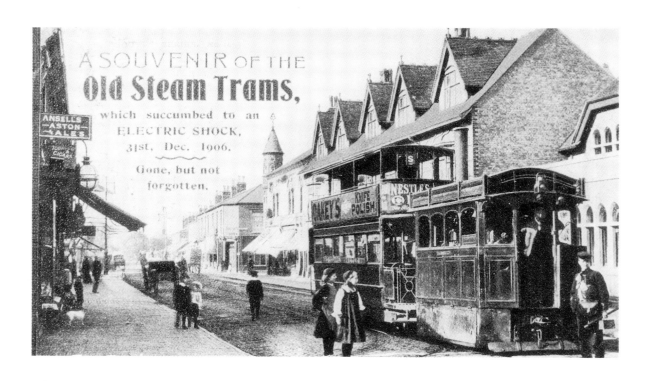

A souvenir postcard of steam trams, the last of which were spirited out of the city on the night of 31 December 1906, to a scrapyard in Wednesbury. The first steam tram routes opened in 1882, and this locomotive was built by Kitson and Co of Leeds.

Moor Street seen from the Bull Ring c1930 at mid-day. Boots was formerly Oswald Bailey's, but all has now disappeared beneath the inner ring road.

Index to Illustrations